I0007851

PYTHON PROGRAMMING

A complete beginners guide
on python machine learning,
data science and tools

Bill Norton

Text Copyright © [Bill Norton]

Legal & Disclaimer

The information contained in this book and its contents is not designed to replace or take the place of any form of medical or professional advice; and is not meant to replace the need for independent medical, financial, legal or other professional advice or services, as may be required. The content and information in this book has been provided for educational and entertainment purposes only.

The content and information contained in this book has been compiled from sources deemed reliable, and it is accurate to the best of the Author's knowledge, information and belief. However, the Author cannot guarantee its accuracy and validity and cannot be held liable for any errors and/or omissions. Further, changes are periodically made to this book as and when needed. Where appropriate and/or necessary, you must consult a professional (including but not limited to your doctor, attorney, financial advisor or such other professional advisor) before using any of the suggested remedies, techniques, or information in this book.

Upon using the contents and information contained in this book, you agree to hold harmless the Author from and against any damages, costs, and expenses, including any legal fees potentially resulting from the application of any of the information provided by this book. This disclaimer applies to any loss, damages or injury caused by the use and application, whether directly or indirectly, of any advice or information presented, whether for breach of contract, tort, negligence, personal injury, criminal intent, or under any other cause of action.

You agree to accept all risks of using the information presented inside this book.

You agree that by continuing to read this book, where appropriate and/or necessary, you shall consult a professional (including but not limited to your doctor, attorney, or financial advisor or such other advisor as needed) before using any of the suggested remedies, techniques, or information in this book.

Table of Contents

Introduction

Python is a programming language that is often recommended for beginners to try messing up things and falling in love with programming. One of the major reasons for the widespread popularity of Python is its simplicity and the power of making things done with less code. Even after the entrance of tens of programming languages in the past decade python doesn't lose its charm and we are pretty confident that is going to stay.

This book is a classical and a layman's introduction to python programming concepts in simple and concise explanations. All the concepts are included with programs so that the reader can understand the essence of the topic.

What is Python?

Python is a programming language that is pretty famous and has a very generous community that produces high-quality projects for various branches of computer science such as Data mining, Machine learning, and Deep learning on a regular basis. It is an old programming language but still solves modern problems perfectly.

This book is not a reference but a smart introduction to python in an easy way. We tried to explain all the concepts in an easy language so that the readers can penetrate the programming concepts in their minds and use them to create some pretty innovative projects.

How to get the most out of this book?

Programming concepts are always understood only if you can practically use them on your own. For this exact reason, we have bundled this book with a lot of programming code examples that will initiate you to code on your own. Already experienced programmers can also use this book as good reference material on python.

There are a lot of books that cover Python in the market but you have chosen us to immerse you into the world of Python programming. We are sure that you will get a good learning experience while reading this book. Let us go!

Chapter 1: What is Python?

This chapter is a comprehensive introduction to python basics and its abilities. We will start with a little history and will then dive into other complex topics. We advise you to use this book both as a reference and learning material.

Python is an explanatory, object-oriented and high-level programming language with dynamic semantics. It can be used as a real cross-platform (running on Linux, macOS, and Windows) language, and its forced indentation syntax makes its code simple and easy to read.

Applications of Python

Python is easier to use than other programming languages. Because Python has a large number of third-party libraries, it is more efficient and faster to use Python to develop application projects. Python is widely used in system management. Multi-national Companies like Industrial Light & Magic use Python to produce special effects in high-budget movies.

Yahoo! is using it (including other technologies) to manage discussion groups. Google uses it to implement many components in web crawlers and search engines. Python is also used in various fields such as computer games and biological information. With the rapid development of artificial intelligence, Python's application has been better popularized.

Python History

Python was founded by Guido van Rossum of the Netherlands. During Thanksgiving Day in 1989, Guido decided to develop a new script interpreter as an inheritance of the ABC language to kill the boredom of Christmas. Python was chosen as the name of the language because he is a fan of BBC TV series "Monty Python's Flying Circus". He wanted to create a mystique about the programming language. For this reason, he named it Python.

Python was born in 1989, but the first public release was issued in 1991, Python2.0 was officially released in October 2000, Python3.0 was officially released in December 2008, and the latest version is Python3.6.5 as of this book is written.

Python is an object-oriented and literal translation computer programming language, as well as a powerful general programming language. It contains a set of perfect and easy-to-understand standard libraries and is supported by a large number of third-party libraries, which can easily accomplish many common tasks.

Its syntax is very simple and clear, unlike most other computer programming languages, it uses a forced indentation to define statement blocks.

Python's Design Style

Python insists on a clear and uniform design style, which makes Python an easy-to-read and easy-to-maintain language that is popular with a large number of users and has a wide range of uses. The general guiding ideology of designers in development is that it is best as long as there is the best way to solve a specific problem.

Python's design philosophy is being elegant, clear, simple and readable.

Python's Object-Oriented philosophy

Python is a programming language that supports object-oriented programming paradigm process. It has a lot of technical abilities that help it to be a better programming language than of procedural languages that are available.

Python developer's philosophy is to use one method, preferably only one method, to do one thing. This is different from most other programming languages. When you are faced with many choices in writing programs in Python, Python developers will usually reject those fancy methods and choose clear, little or no ambiguous syntax. These criteria are what we usually call Python's maxim.

You can see a famous article written by Tim Peters on python basics. It introduces some important principles that need to be paid attention to when writing beautiful Python programs, to understand Python's design philosophy. Also, you can refer to relevant websites to learn about Python's design philosophy.

In the next section, we will discuss installing third-party libraries in Python language. This is a basic skill that is necessary for python programmers to learn before dealing with hard coding skills. It is pretty basic and very useful for beginners. Let us learn about it in detail.

How to install the third-party libraries?

Python has a powerful standard library, and the Python community provides a large number of third-party libraries in a similar way to the standard library. If strong standard libraries have laid for the foundation for Python's development, third party libraries are responsible for Python's continuous development. With continuous updates of Python, some stable third-party libraries have been added to the standard library.

When Anaconda was installed, Python's standard libraries and some commonly used third-party libraries were installed with a Python interpreter. You can enter "pip list" at the Windows prompt to view the installed libraries. All the installed libraries will then appear on the output screen.

If you want to use a third-party library that is not installed, you must install it using the installation method described below. Beginners can skip this now if it is too overwhelming to concentrate on. You can always come back to this section for understanding the installation of third-party modules.

1) Source installation

Many third-party libraries are open source, almost all of which can be found on GitHub or PyPI. Most of the source codes found are available in zip, tar.zip, tar.bz2 format compression packages. After unpacking these compressed packages, you will usually see a setup.py file. Open the Windows command line window and enter the folder.

Run the following command to install:

run setup.py // This is the usually used command

2) Package Manager

Many programming languages now have package managers, such as Ruby's gem and nodejs's npm. Python is certainly no exception. Pip and conda can be used to install third-party libraries.

(1) pip Management of Python Library.

You should remember that when Python installation was introduced earlier, one of the options that it offers was to install the pip Package Manager. Of course, if Anaconda is selected for installation it should be noted that the package manager has already installed it automatically. If the pip package manager has been installed, enter pip on the command line and click enter, and you can see the results.

pip {Enter the third-party name}

When installing a third-party library using the pip installation module, the system will automatically download the installation file.

For example, install the flask framework with the following command:

pip install flask

Command to Uninstall Installed Third-Party Libraries

pip uninstall {Enter third party name here} □

If you want to view the installed libraries, including those that come with the system and those that are installed manually, you only need to execute the command 'pip all'.

More pip parameters and functions can be viewed by entering "pip" on the command line interface.

(2) Condo's management of Python libraries.

Conda can be installed by installing Minconda or Anaconda, which is a simplified version of python and that only contains conda and its dependencies. Conda's management of Python libraries is much the same as pip's. Currently, the main commands that can be used are to install, uninstall and view the installed libraries.

conda {Enter the command here}

For more information about the use of conda, interested readers can use relevant materials from online for study.

With this, we have completed a brief introduction to Python. In the next chapter, we will discuss some of the specialties of Python when compared with other programming languages. We will also learn about the working process of Python in detail in the next chapter. Follow along!

Chapter 2: Differences between Python and other programming languages?

Python is an interpretive, object-oriented and dynamic data type high-level programming language. Since the birth of Python language in the early 1990s, it has gradually been widely used in processing system management tasks and Web programming. Especially with the continuous development of artificial intelligence, Python has become one of the most popular programming languages.

Why is Python special?

There are hundreds of programming languages now available for programmers to start with. However, according to statistics from a survey done by Harvard computer scientists Python is a leading language among beginners. We will in this section discuss about some of the reasons that make Python an understandable language for new programmers.

Python has the following major advantages over other programming languages:

(1) The grammar is concise and clear, and the code is highly readable. Python's syntax requires mandatory indentation, which is used to reflect the logical relationship between statements and significantly improve the readability of the program.

(2) Because it is simple and clear, it is also a programming language with high development efficiency.

(3) Python can be truly cross-platform, for example, the programs we develop can run on Windows, Linux, macOS systems. This is its portability advantage.

(4) It consists of A large number of rich libraries or extensions. Python is often nicknamed glue language. It can easily connect

various modules written in other languages, especially C/C++. Using these abundant third-party libraries, we can easily develop our applications.

(5) The amount of code is small, which improves the software quality to a certain extent. Since the amount of code written in Python is much smaller than that in other languages, the probability of errors is much smaller, which improves the quality of the software written to a certain extent.

Python is very versatile and can be used in the following areas:

(1) web page development;

(2) Visual (GUI) interface development;

(3) Network (can be used for network programming);

(4) System programming;

(5) Data analysis;

(6) Machine learning (Python has various libraries to support it);

(7) Web crawlers (such as those used by Google);

(8) Scientific calculation (Python is used in many aspects of the scientific calculation).

For example, Python is used in many Google services. YouTube is also implemented in Python. The basic framework of the Wikipedia Network initially is also implemented in Python.

How does python work?

Python Program Execution Principle is very simple. We all know that programs written in compiled languages such as C/C++ need to be converted from source files to machine languages used by computers, and then binary executable files are formed after linking by linkers. When running the program, you can load the binary program from the hard disk into memory and run it.

However, for Python, Python source code does not need to be compiled into binary code. It can run programs directly from the source code. The Python interpreter converts the source code into bytecode and then forwards the compiled bytecode to the Python virtual machine (PVM) for execution.

When we run the Python program, the Python interpreter performs two steps.

(1) Compiles Source Code into Byte Code

Compiled bytecode is a Python-specific expression. It is not a binary machine code and needs further compilation before it can be executed by the machine. This is also why Python code cannot run as fast as C/C++.

If the Python process has to write permission on the machine, it will save the bytecode of the program as a file with the extension .pyc. If Python cannot write the bytecode on the machine, the bytecode will be generated in memory and automatically discarded at the end of the program. When building a program, it is best to give Python permission to write on the computer, so as long as the source code is unchanged, the generated .py file can be reused to improve the execution efficiency.

(2) Forwarding the compiled bytecode to Python Virtual Machine (PVM) for execution.

PVM is short for Python Virtual Machine. It is Python's running engine and part of the Python system. It is a large loop that iteratively runs bytecode instructions, completing operations one after another.

In this process, every python program is executed and gives results that can be further analyzed and tested to completely deploy as new applications.

What to look forward to?

As said before, it is always tough to learn a programming language from scratch. Python is one of the most popular programming languages for beginners because it is straight to the point without any deviations. A lot of code is very simple and does what you say. It is comfortably easy for beginners to create predictive logics using python. All we are asking you to do is to stick consistently with python and you can do wonders with it. We recommend you to check GitHub python programs to further increase your interest in Python programming.

In the next chapter, we will in detail discuss about the installation procedure of Python in different operating systems. Let us go!

Chapter 3: How to install Python on your PC?

In the previous chapters, we have discussed Python from a technical and theoretical perspective. From the next chapter, we will start discussing various lexical concepts that make python what it is. Before discussing all those concepts, we need to first install Python in our system. This chapter is a tutorial that explains to you how to install Python in different operating systems. Let us start!

Python Installation and Operation

Due to Python's cross-platform feature, Windows, Linux and macOS systems all support Python's software installation. First of all, we need to download the installation software.

1. Download Python

Here we introduce the installation and operation of Python under the Windows environment. Since there is no built-in Python environment in the Windows operating system, it needs to be installed independently. The installation package can be downloaded from Python's official website (www.Python.org). After opening the official website search for the navigation bar that has a "Downloads" button.

The website recommends a link by default because it can detect your operating system and recommend the latest version of Python 3.x, 3.6.5. After entering the download page of the corresponding version, there is a basic introduction to the environment you are trying to download. Several different versions are mainly aimed at different operating system platforms.

You can choose different files to download according to whether your system is 32-bit or 64-bit.

In the new page that opens, we can find other versions, including the latest test version and the required version 3.4. If you want to install a 64-bit version of 3.6.5, click the framed link on the current page.

At the bottom of the newly opened page, we can find several other links. The file that starts with the Windows entity represents the 64-bit version of Windows, while the file that does not include 64 represents the 32-bit version.

The website shows a compressed installation package (Windows x86-64 Embedded ZipFile), an executable installation file, and a Web-based installation file (Windows x86-64). It is most convenient to download the executable installation package.

Note: 64-bit version cannot be installed on a 32-bit system, but a 32-bit version can be installed on a 32-bit system or 64-bit system.

2. Install Python

The Windows executable installation package is easier to install. Just like installing other Windows applications, we just need to select the appropriate option and click "Next" to complete the installation.

When the options appear in the installation, do not rush to the next step (the system demonstrated here is 64-bit in itself).

It must be noted that after "Add Python3.6 to PATH" is checked and Python 3.6 is added to the environment variable, Python's interactive prompt or Python's commands can be started directly and conveniently at the Windows command prompt in the future.

After selecting "Add Python 3.6 to PATH", select custom installation. Of course, it is also possible to select the first item for installation, which means Python is installed in the user directory of C disk. But at this time, you'd better know what the user directory is so that you can find the installed Python.exe files when necessary in the future.

Proceed with the instructions and python will be installed successfully in the system.

3. Start Python

Python can be started in two ways.

1) Start Python's Own IDLE

If you want to run Python, you can click the "start" button on the Windows desktop and enter "IDLE" in the search box that appears to launch a Python desktop application to quickly provide a prompt of "read-evaluate-print-loop".

IDLE is Python's own simple IDE (Integrated Development Environment), which is Python's graphical interface editor. IDLE can be regarded as a simple version of an integrated development environment. Its function looks simple, but it is helpful for beginners to learn the Python language itself.

Here, a REPL environment is provided, that is, it reads the user's input ("Read"), returns to the car, evaluates and calculates ("Evaluate"), then prints the result ("Print"), and then a prompt "Loop" appears, thus circulating.

2) Start Python at Windows Prompt

Another way to start Python is to run Python programs through the Windows command prompt, and enter "cmd" in the Windows search box (or press "Win+R" key to open the run prompt box, note the "Win" key on the keyboard), or click the start button to enter "cmd" in the pop-up search box and enter to start the Windows command line window.

Note: the flashing cursor after ">" seen here is the command prompt provided by Windows.

When installing Python, since the "Add Python 3.6 to PATH" option is checked and the installed Python is added to the environment variable of Windows, Python can be successfully started by entering "python" after the prompt ">".

The prompt "> > >" indicates that Python installation was successful and Python has been started. The prompt "> > >" is Python-specific.

Next, "print("Hello Python!" is executed in either the first or second startup mode.) ".

If you want to return to the Windows command prompt, you can reach the goal by pressing the shortcut key "Ctrl+Z".

The above two methods are both REPL forms, suitable for writing relatively short programs or commands, and have the advantages of simplicity and flexibility. If the program has more functions and more modules or packages are called, the REPL form is not very convenient to maintain.

In this chapter, we have explained about Installation of Python in detail. In the next chapters, we will start discussing Python syntax in detail. Follow along!

Chapter 4: Python Data types

Python and other programming languages use data types to store values logically in memory. Distinguishing data with values can help operations perform faster. We will also discuss other important programming concepts such as identifiers and reserved keywords in this chapter. Follow along!

Let's start with a detailed discussion of data types.

The operations supported by an object and its description are determined by the data type. Therefore, learning about datatypes is very important for programmers. The Python language provides several built-in data types with rich functions.

Before explaining each data type and its supported operations, the type of the object is usually checked. Python provides a specific built-in function type () to perform these operations. It returns a special type called a type object, which can be divided into other types.

Type detection function [type ()]

Use the type () function to quickly check the type of a variable or to determine the type of operation they can perform.

For example:

type(example)

// Where example =8

We will get the output as int by the type () function.

The Type () function is very simple. It can quickly help us detect the actual type of an object, whether by the name or value of a variable.

Empty object (None)

Another special type in Python is called an empty object. It is just empty and can hold null values.

Simple numeric types

Integer

Integer type (int) is simply an integer, which is used to represent an integer, for example, 100, 2016, etc. Integer literals are represented in four ways: decimal, binary (beginning with "0B" or "0b"), octal (beginning with the number "0") and hexadecimal (beginning with "0X" or "0x").

Python's integer can represent a limited range, which is consistent with the system's maximum integer. For example, the integer on a 32-bit computer is 32 bits, and the range of numbers that can be represented is 231 ~ 2311. Integers on 64-bit computers are 64-bit, and the range of numbers that can be represented is 263 ~ 2631.

Next, look at some examples of integer code, as follows:

first=231283

```
type(first)
```

```
<type 'int'>
```

```
first
```

```
231283
```

In the above code, the value of the variable first in line1 code is a binary integer, which belongs to int type. This has been verified in the next lines. Lines 4 to 5 directly output the value of first, and the result is 231283.

Decimal numbers can be converted to binary, octal or hexadecimal using the specified function.

The sample code is as follows:

```
bin (20) # converts decimal 20 to binary
```

```
'0b10100'
```

```
oct (20) # converts decimal 20 to octal
```

```
'o024'
```

```
hex (20) # convert decimal 20 to hexadecimal
```

```
'0x14'
```

Long Integer

Long is a superset of integers, which can represent an infinite integer (actually only limited by the computer's virtual memory size). Long integer literal values are followed by the letters "l" or "l" (uppercase "l" is recommended). Long and integer operations are the same.

The sample code is as follows:

```
first=13798433*3749803498
```

```
<type 'long'>
```

In the long run, integer and long integer are gradually unified into an integer type. Starting from Python 2.3, integer overflow errors will no longer be reported, and the results will be automatically converted to long integers. Now the two types of integers can be said to be seamlessly combined, and the long integer suffix "L" becomes optional.

Floating point type

Float is used to represent real numbers. For example, 3.14, 9.19, etc. are all floating-point types. Floating-point literals can be expressed in decimal or scientific notation.

The scientific notation in Python is expressed as follows:

< real number > e or e < integer >

Wherein, e or e represents a base of 10, the following integer represents an index, and the positive and negative of the index are expressed by+or, where+can be omitted. For example, 1.34E3 means 1.34×10^3 and 1.5E−3 means 1.5×10-3.

The sample code is as follows:

> > 1.2e5 # floating-point number is 1.2×10^5

One hundred and twenty thousand

Boolean type

The boolean type can be regarded as a special integer. Boolean data has only two values: True and False, corresponding to 1 and 0 of integer respectively. Every Python object is inherently boolean (True or False), which can then be used in boolean tests (such as if, while).

User-defined class instances that return 0 or False if methods nonzero () or len () are defined. Boolean values of all objects except the above objects are True. This section involves a lot of knowledge explained later. All you need to know here is that Boolean values can only be True and False.

plural

The complex number type is used to represent the complex number in mathematics. For example, 5+3j and −3.4−6.8j are all complex number types. The plural type in Python is a data type that is not available in general computer languages.

It has the following two characteristics:

(1) Complex numbers consist of real numbers and imaginary numbers, which are expressed as real+imagj or real+imagJ.

(2) The real part and imaginary part imag of complex numbers are both floating-point types.

It should be noted that a complex number must have real numbers and j representing imaginary parts, e.g. 1j and 1j are complex numbers, and 0.0 is not a complex number, and the real part representing imaginary parts cannot be omitted even if it is 1.

Example codes for complex numbers are as follows:

sample = 6+2j

sample

(6+2j)

sample.real # real part

One

type(sample.real)

<class 'float'>

sample.imag # imaginary part

Two

type(sample.imag)

<class 'float'>

Identifiers and keywords

identifier

In real life, people often use some names to mark things. For example, each fruit has a name to mark.

Similarly, if you want to express something in a program, you need developers to customize some symbols and names, which are called identifiers. For example, variable names, function names, etc. are identifiers.

The identifier in Python consists of letters, numbers and underscore "_", and its naming method needs to follow certain rules, as follows.

(1) Identifiers consist of letters, underscores, and numbers, and cannot begin with numbers.

The sample code is as follows:

FromNo12 # legal identifier

From#12 # is an illegal identifier. Identifiers cannot contain # symbols.

2ndObj # is an illegal identifier. Identifiers cannot start with a number.

(2) Identifiers in Python are case sensitive. For example, andy and Andy are different identifiers.

(3) Identifiers in Python cannot use keywords. For example, if cannot be used as an identifier.

Also, to standardize the naming of identifiers, the following suggestions are made on the naming of identifiers.

(1) Knowing the meaning by name: give a meaningful name and try your best to know what the identifier means at a glance, thus improving the readability of the code. For example, the definition name is represented by name, and the definition student is represented by student.

(2) When naming variables, many computer languages suggest hump naming. However, hump naming is not recommended in Python.

keywords

In Python, identifiers with special functions are called keywords. The keyword is already used by Python itself, and developers are not allowed to define identifiers with the same name as the keyword.

The keywords in Python each represent a different meaning. If you want to view the keyword information, you can enter the help () command to enter the help system to view.

The sample code is as follows:

> > > help () # enter the help system

Help> keywords # view all keyword lists

Help> return # view the description of the keyword return

Help > quit # to exit the help system

With this we have completed a brief explanation to data types and in the next chapter we will explain about variables in detail. Follow along!

Chapter 5: Python Variables

Programming is a tough task and it requires hard work to master various topics. Programmers are destined to know about how computers store data. This will make it easy to understand their resources and successfully pool data types to create favorable applications. This may seem silly for programs with fewer lines of code but when you are using advanced third-party libraries to create complex applications this will become essential. In the previous chapter we have talked about data types in detail and in this chapter we will in detail discuss variables that store data for repetitive usage.

Variables

In real life, when we buy things in supermarkets, we often need to use shopping carts to store items. After all, after items are purchased, we can check out at the cash register.

Let's imagine, if you want to sum up multiple data in the program, you need to store the data first and then add up the data.

In Python, variables are needed to store data. Variables can be understood as shopping carts used for shopping in supermarkets, and their types and values are initialized at the moment of assignment. The assignment of variables is represented by an equal sign, and the example code is shown below. We will also discuss in detail about Assignment operation in the next chapter.

Num1 = 257 # Num1 is a variable, just like a shopping cart, which stores data 257

Num2 = 87 # Num2 is also a variable, and the stored data is 87

Result = num1+num2 # Accumulates the data in the two "shopping carts" num1 and num2 and then puts them into the result variable

In the above example, num1, num2, and result are variables. Among them, variables num1 and num2 are just like a shopping cart, and the data they store are 257 and 87 respectively. The data stored in the variable result is the cumulative sum of the data in the two "shopping carts" num1 and num2.

Types of Variables

Variables are used to store data, so have you ever thought about how much space we should let variables take up and what kind of data to store? Before explaining the types of variables, let's take a look at an example of life.

For example, we need to transport a computer. Large trucks and cars can be completed. However, if we use a large truck to transport a computer, it is a little fussy and wastes the space of a large truck.

Similarly, if variables are used to store data, in order to make full use of memory space, we can specify different types for variables.

(1) Number Type

Number types in Python include integer, floating-point, and complex types.

The sample code is as follows:

x = 1

x = 3.232

x = 5.65f

(2) Boolean type

Boolean type is a special integer with only two values, True and False. If a Boolean value is evaluated numerically, True will be treated as integer 1 and False as integer 0.

(3) String Type

A string in Python is defined as a collection of characters that are enclosed in quotation marks, which can be single, double quotation marks, or triple quotation marks (three consecutive single quotation marks or double quotation marks). The string has index rules, the index of the first character is 0, the index of the second character is 1, and so on.

The following is a sample code for a string:

Str1='God'

Str2="This is great"

Str3="'You are lost'"

(4) List and tuple type

We can think of lists and tuples as ordinary "arrays". They can hold any number of values of any type, which are called elements. The difference is that the elements in the list are contained in brackets []. The number and value of elements can be modified at will. The elements in the tuple are contained in parentheses (). Elements cannot be modified.

Let's look at the representation of lists and tuples.

A list = [1,768,' lost'] # This is a list

A tuple = (1,2464,' great') # This is a tuple

(5) dictionary type

Dictionary is a mapping data type in Python and consists of key-value pairs. Dictionaries can store different types of elements, which are contained in braces {}. In general, the keys of the dictionary will be expressed in the form of strings or numbers, and the values can be of any type.

The sample code is as follows:

Sample = {"name": "Rob", "age": 67} # this is a dictionary

In the above code, the variable Sample is a dictionary type, which stores two elements, the key of the first element is a name, and the value is Rob. The key of the second element is age with a value of 67.

In Python, as long as a variable is defined and the variable stores data, the data type of the variable is already determined. This is because the system will automatically identify the data type of the variable, and there is no need for developers to explicitly specify the data type of the variable.

If you want to view the type of a variable, you can use "Type" (the name of the variable).

The sample code is as follows:

>>> dude = 5.234

> > > type (dude)//use the type function to view types

In the above code, the value stored in the variable num is 5.234, and the system will automatically judge the data type of num variable as float according to the value. Therefore, when viewing the data type of variable num using the type function, the result is float.

In the next section, we will discuss some of the syntactical rules to be followed while writing code such as comments and sentence wrapping.

What are comments in Python?

The single-line comment in Python starts with #, and the sample code is as follows:

This is the start

print ("Hello, This is the end!") # Second comment

A multiline comment can use three quotation marks as the opening and closing symbols, and the three quotation marks can be three single quotation marks or three double quotation marks. For example, when entering the declaration file of the print function, the relevant explanations of the print function are all annotated with three quotation marks.

''' Comment here ''' # Single quotation comment

""" Comment here """ # Double quotation comment

Lines and indents

Python's most important and well-discussed ability is that it uses different forms of indentation, without using braces {}.

The sample code is as follows:

if {Enter the Boolean entity here}

Print ("This is right") # Get use of a placeholder

else:

Print ("This is wrong") # Get use of a placeholder

The above program is indented with an inconsistent number of spaces, which will lead to running errors.

 if {Enter the Boolean entity here}

 print ("get this")

 print ("This is right")

else:

 print ("Do this")

PRINT ("This is wrong") # Inconsistent indentations will result in running errors

Due to inconsistent indentation of the above programs, indentation error will appear after execution.

Note:

(1) For a person who uses indentation as a code block for the first time, he may be confused about the width of indentation. Here, we recommend using 4 spaces.

(2) Tabs represent different blank widths in different text editors. If the code we use is to be used across platforms, it is recommended that you do not use tabs.

Sentence Wrapping

Python usually writes a statement one line at a time, but if it is syntactically too long, it needs line wrapping, which can be implemented by adding a pair of parentheses to the outside of the statement.

Now we are ready to give a brief explanation about various essential programming operations in the next chapter. Let us start with it!

Chapter 6: Basic operation of Python Language

In the previous chapters, we have discussed various lexical concepts that are necessary to write efficient code. In this chapter, we will discuss various operations that made Python a popular language. This is a comprehensive chapter and introduces you to a lot of concepts in detail. Let us start!

What is a statement?

When a variable is declared, an expression is used to create and process the object. If some logical control is added, a statement is formed. It can also be said that statements contain expressions, so statements are the most basic infrastructure for Python programs.

Python Assignment Statement

Learning assignment statements in Python makes it easier to learn the other statements. Learning Python assignment statement is mainly to master and understand its logic.

1. Assignment statement

The essence of assignment statements in Python is to create a reference to an object.

There are mainly the following methods of an assignment.

a) Basic assignment method

☐ "first=5"

This is equivalent to creating a variable first that points to the object 5 stored in memory. "first=5" is an assignment statement. After performing the assignment operation, you can print or display the value of first at will.

2) Understand assignment logic

When declaring variables, there are at least two parts, one is the variable table used to store variable names, and the other is the memory storage area [4,6].

When "first=5" is declared, the system first opens a storage space in the memory area, stores the value 5, and then points the variable first to the object 5 stored in the memory, which is equivalent to having the object 5 first in the memory storage area. Then first appears in the variable table, and points to 5. This point can also be called "reference".

Although the syntax of assignment statements is simple, please carefully understand the assignment logic in Python. This kind of assignment logic affects all aspects of Python. If you understand assignment logic, you can better understand and write Python programs.

If you have programming experience in C language, you will know that variables in C programs hold value, while variables in Python point to a value. Variables exist only as a reference relationship and no longer have storage functions. In Python, each data occupies a memory space, and data is called an object in Python.

An integer 5 is an int object, a' hello' is a string object, and a [1, 2, 3] is a list object.

In Python, you can use the global built-in function id(obj) to obtain the id of an object as the storage address of the object in memory. The global built-in function is used directly and does not need to refer to any package.

☐ Note: The change of address before and after variable first indicates that the variable points to the object!

After an object is created, it cannot be destroyed directly. Therefore, in the above example, the variable a points to the object 5 first, and then continues to execute "a=a+5", which produces a new object 10. Since the object 5 cannot be destroyed, let A point to the new object 10 instead of overwriting the object 5 with the object 10. After the code execution is completed, there are still objects 5 and 10 in the memory, but the variable A points to the new object 10.

If no variable points to object 5 (it cannot be referenced), Python will use a garbage collection mechanism to decide whether to recycle it (this is automatic and does not require the programmer to worry about it).

There is a garbage collection mechanism inside Python. The garbage collection mechanism detects that if no variable references an object within a specific time, the object will be collected, releasing the resources it occupies.

There is a reference counter inside Python, and the garbage collection mechanism judges whether an object has a reference according to the reference counter, to decide whether to automatically release the resources occupied by the object. The garbage collection mechanism targets unreferenced objects in Python and is inferred from a result obtained by a reference counter.

This understanding is also very important. When we talk about data types such as lists in the future, we will see again the importance of correctly understanding the variable pointing to the object.

Multi-objective assignment

The multi-objective assignment is a way of assigning the same value to multiple variables.

☐ Enhanced assignment or parameterized assignment

Sometimes it is desirable to replace the original value of a variable by re-assigning it after doing an operation based on its original value.

☐ Exchange the values of two variables.

In other languages, such as Java, C, C++, etc., at least three lines of code are required to exchange the values of two variables, while in Python, only one line of code is required to exchange the values of two variables.

Before introducing other Python statements, let us look at the sequential execution and basic input and output in Python process control.

Sequential execution is the default code execution method in process control and is relatively simple. The basic principle is that the sequence of code execution is consistent with the sequence of program code writing.

The program execution order is consistent with the writing order.

The data in the above program is fixed in the program, but sometimes it may be necessary for programmers or software users to input some data into the program during the operation of the program, which requires input functions.

input () function

Input on the console is realized through the global function input (). The input () function receives information input from the console by the user. The default type is a str character type, which can be converted into specific data types as required.

If you want to give the user some hints when inputting data, you can pass in a parameter with hints in the input () function!

eval () function

The eval () function evaluates str character data as a valid expression and returns the result. Simply put, it is to remove the quotation marks at the left and right ends of the string.

print () function

The print () function here simply outputs the value of an object or variable. The print () function has some commonly used parameters, which are very flexible to use in actual development.

If you want to use a special line of characters to separate the output of the front and back lines, such as 20 "=" to separate the output of the front and back lines, you can use "print("="*20)" to achieve the goal.

☐ 1) Multiple variables are output on one line, separated by spaces by default Outputs multiple contents separated by commas on one line, with the separator being a space.

2) Multiple variables are output on one line, and the separator between them is changed

If you want the output to be separated by other separators, you can write a delimiter statement. Any character can be used as the delimiter here, that is, the print () function can specify the delimiter manually.

Multiple lines of print () function output on one line

In the parameter table of the print () function, there is a parameter "end" that specifies the termination symbol. by default, it is a line break, that is, "end='\n'". Therefore, the output of multiple print statements can be output on one line by specifying a terminator.

☐ The default delimiter for the print () function is a space, and the terminating symbol is a newline' \n'. After understanding the above contents, the flexibility of output will be greatly improved in actual development.

Digital print format

Specify the format or number of digits of the output number by formatting the string.

1) Outputs decimals of specified digits

☐ In the print format, the ':' in curly brackets indicates that the value appearing at the current position is formatted, and the' .2f' indicates that the following value is output as floating-point, but only 2 decimal places are reserved, and the third digit is rounded.

2) output a fixed width value

If you want to specify the width of the overall digital output, the form is as follows:

width {Enter value}

☐ Note:' {:12, .2f}' means the total width, which is aligned to the right by default, with not enough digits, and is preceded by a space; ", "means thousands separator; ".2f" means keeping 2 decimal places.

☐ Because sometimes it is necessary to output multiple lines of content on the console, and each line has multiple columns, but each line has a length and a short length. If you want to typeset more neatly, you can use this method at this time.

For more usage of the print () function, please refer to it through the help(print) command.

With this, we have completed a comprehensive chapter that explained to us a lot of python programming concepts. In the next chapter, we will in detail discuss modules that give interactivity to python. Let us go!

Chapter 7: Interactivity in Python

Python is a thorough language that utilizes a lot of components. However, you need to remember that one of the most important reasons for the success of Python is its interactivity. Every programming language provides interactivity using different methodologies. Python is however known to provide interactivity with the help of modules and packages. In this chapter, we will discuss these functions in detail along with a lot of examples. Follow along!

How Modules provide interactivity?

In Python, the import keyword can be used to introduce a module. For example, the math module can be introduced and import math can be used.

The basic format for introducing modules using import is as follows:

import firstmodule,secondmodule...

At this time, if the module is located at that same location, the module will be imported automatically.

If you want to call a function in a module, you must reference it like this:

Module Name. {Enter the name of the function}

When calling a function in a module, the module name is added because there may be functions with the same name in multiple modules. At this time, if only the function name is used to call, the interpreter cannot know which function to call. Therefore, if a module is introduced as described above, the calling function must be added with the module name.

Specific examples are as follows:

import math

This is said to be wrong

print(sqrt(12))

Only in this way can the results be correctly output

print({Enter the module here}.sqrt(12))

Sometimes we only need to use a certain function in the module, and only need to introduce the function. At this time, the following format can be applied:

from {Name of the entity} import function name 1, function name 2 ..

For your clear understanding here is an instance:

from fib import {Enter the Fibonacci instance here}

When introducing a function in this way, only the function name and not the module name can be given when calling the function, but when two modules contain functions with the same name, the latter introduction will cover the previous introduction.

That is to say, if there is a function function in module A, there is also a function function in module B. If the function in A is introduced before the function in B, then when the function is called, the function in module B is executed.

You can also use the following statement for invoking all statements at once.

From module name import *

It should be noted that although Python provides a simple method to import all items in a module you should use other invoking statements too.

When we use import to introduce a module, how does the Python interpreter find the corresponding file?

This involves Python's search path, which consists of a series of directory names, from which Python interpreter searches for the introduced modules in turn.

The search path is determined when Python is compiled or installed, and the installation of the new library should also be modified.

The search operation to the PATH variable in the sys module is used, and can be verified by code as follows:

import provider

print(provider.path)

Now, create a fibo.py file in the interpreter's current directory or a directory in sys.path, with the following sample code:

fibonacci Sequence Module

deffib (n): # fibonacci sequence defined to n

first, second = 0, 1

while second < n:

print(second, end=' ')

```
first, second = second, first+second
print()
def fib2 (n): # Fibonacci sequence returned to n
result = []
first, second = 0, 1
while second < n:
result.append(second)
first, second = second, first+second
return result
```

Then enter the Python interpreter and import this module using the following command:

```
import fibo
```

In doing so, the name of the function directly defined in fibo is not written into the current symbol table, but the name of the module fibo is written there. You can use the module name to access the function, with the following sample code:

```
import fibo
fibo.fib(1000)
fibo.fib2(100)
fibo.__name__
```

If you plan to use a function frequently, you can assign it to a local name.

The example code is as follows:

```
fib=fibo.fib
fib(500)
```

□ *Module production*

In Python, each Python file can be used as a module, and the name of the module is the name of the file. At this time, if you want to use the test.py file in the main.py file, you can use "from test import add" to introduce it.

Example main.py

```
from test import add
result = test.add(11,22)
print(result)
```

In actual development, after a developer has written a module, to make the module achieve the desired effect in the project, the developer will add some test information to the py file.

At this time, if this file is introduced into other py files, think about whether the code tested will also execute? The test file is introduced into main.py the sample code is as follows:

As can be seen from the above results, the test code in test.py is also running. However, this is not reasonable. Test code should only be run when test.py is executed separately, and should not be executed when referenced by other files.

To solve this problem, Python provides a special attribute. Each module has a special attribute. when its value is' __main__', it indicates that the module itself is running, otherwise, it is referenced. Therefore, if we want a program block in the module not to execute when the module is introduced, we can do so by judging the value of the __name__ attribute.

Packages

To organize the modules well, multiple modules are usually put into one package. The package is the directory where Python module files are located, and __init__.py files must exist under the directory (the file contents can be empty).

At this time, if main.py wants to reference module_a1 in package_a, it can be implemented with the following statement:

```
from package_a import module_a1
import package_a.module_a1
```

With this, we have completed a brief explanation of interactivity in python using modules. In the next chapter, we will talk about structures in detail. Follow along!

Chapter 8: Structures in Python

Python is a structural language and provides various structures to store and manipulate data for performing operations. In this chapter, we will in detail discuss structures such as lists. A lot of this chapter is theoretical and needs an understanding of various concepts explained before. Let us start!

What is a list?

The string data type learned earlier can be used to store a single piece string of information. But Suppose if there are 100 students in a class. If you want to store the names of all the students in this class, you need to define 100 variables, and each variable stores one student's name.

However, if there are 1,000 students or more, what should we do?

You are lucky because structures such as lists can solve the above problem. A list is a data structure in Python that can store different types of data. The way to create the list is very simple, just use square brackets to enclose the different data items separated by commas.

The sample code is as follows:

A = [1,'Tom','a', [2, 'b']]

As the index of strings, the list index starts from 0. We can access the values in the list by subscript index.

Example Accessing List Elements Using Indexes

A = ['Tom', 'Sam, 'Ram']

print(A[0])

```
print(A[1])
```

```
print(A[2])
```

In Example, an index is used to access elements in the list, where the index of the first element is 0, the index of the second element is 1, and so on.

To output each data of the list more efficiently, we can use the for and while loops to traverse the output list.

The following is a case study to illustrate how to loop through the list using for and while.

1. Use the for loop to traverse the list

The way to use the for loop to traverse the list is very simple, just need to traverse the list as a sequence in the for-loop expression.

Next, a case will be presented to understand this scenario.

```
getdetails = ['Sam','Tom','Ram']
```

```
for name in getdetails:
```

```
print(name)
```

In Example, when using the for loop to traverse the list, since the list is originally a sequence, the names list can be directly used as the sequence of the for-loop expression to obtain the elements in the list one by one.

2. Use while loop to traverse the list

To use the while loop to traverse the list, first, you need to obtain the length of the list, and use the obtained list length as the condition of the while loop.

Next, a case will be presented, as shown in Example.

Example: Uses the while loop to traverse the list

```
getdetails = ['Sam','Tom','Ram']
```

```
length = len(namesList)
```

```
first = 0
```

```
while first<length:
```

```
print(namesList[first])
```

```
first+=1
```

In Example, when using the while loop to traverse the list, because the while loop needs to specify the number of traversals, it is necessary to use the len function to obtain the length of the list, that is, the number of elements to traverse.

List Common Operations

Add Elements to the List

There are many ways to add elements to the list, as follows:

(1) You can add elements to the list through append.

(2) extend allows you to add elements from another list to the list one by one.

(3) insert the element object before the specified position index by insert(index, object).

Next, we will demonstrate the use of these methods through case studies as follows.

1. Add elements to the list by append

Elements added to the list using append are at the end of the list. Next, we will demonstrate it through a case, as shown in Example.

Prompt and Add Element

temp = input ('please enter the name of the student to be added:')

A.append(temp)

In the example, the program uses append to add an element at the end of the list and uses for loop to traverse the list before and after adding the element, respectively, to verify whether the element in the list was added successfully.

2. Add elements to the list through extend

Use extend to add all elements from one list to another. Next, a case will be presented.

Examples Use extend to Add List Elements

first = [1, 2]

second = [3, 4]

first.append(second)

print(first)

first.extend(second)

print(first)

In Examples, append is used to add List first to the end of List second, and then extend is used to add all the elements of List B to List A.

3. Add elements to the list by insert

Use insert to add an element at a specified location in the list. Next, a case will be presented, as shown in Example.

Example Use insert to insert an element into a list

sample = [0, 1, 2]

sample.insert(1, 3)

print(sample)

In Example, the second line of code uses insert to add an element 3 to the list at index 1.

Find Elements in List

The so-called lookup is to see if the specified element exists. Common operators for lookup in Python are explained below.

(1)in (present): if present, the result is True; otherwise, it is False.

(2)not in: If it does not exist, the result is True, otherwise it is False.

Next, a case is used to demonstrate how to find elements in the list.

Example Finding Elements in a List

findName = input ('please enter the name you want to find:')

look for existence

if findName in {Enter entity details here}

In the example, through the traversal of the list, find out whether the specified element exists in the list. After the program is run, two kinds of results will be generated, and the results of these two operations are shown.

Delete Elements from the List

In real life, if a student changes classes, then the transferred student information should be deleted. The deletion function is often used in development. There are three common deletion methods for list elements, as follows.

(1)del: Delete according to subscript.

(2)pop: Take away the end element

(3)remove: Remove according to the value of the element.

Next, we will demonstrate the use of the above three deletion methods through cases as follows.

1. Use del to delete the list

Del can be used to delete the entire list. Next, we will demonstrate it through a case.

Examples Use del to Delete Elements in a List

del movieName[2]

2. Use pop to delete list elements

Pop can be used to delete the last element of the list. Next, a case will be presented.

movieName.pop()

3. Use remove to remove list elements

Use remove to remove a specified element of the list. Next, we will demonstrate it through a case.

movieName.remove ('lord of the rings')

Sorting Operation of List

If you want to rearrange the elements in the list, you can use the sort or reverse method. Among them, the sort method rearranges the elements in the list in a specific order. The reverse method is to reverse the list. Next, a case is used to demonstrate the use of these two methods.

Example: Sorting Operation of List

sample = [1, 4, 2, 3]

sample.reverse()

sample.sort()

print(sample)

In the example, the second line of codes arranges the list in reverse order, the fourth line of codes arranges the list recursively, and the sixth line of codes arranges the list from large to small.

With this, we have completed various operations that structures can perform. In the next chapter, we will in detail discuss functions with various examples. Let us go!

Chapter 9: Functions in Python

This chapter is a comprehensive guide about functions. We will look at various components of function with examples. Let us go!

What is a Function?

Functions are organized and reusable code segments used to implement single or associated functionalities, which can improve the modularity of applications and the reuse rate of codes. Python provides many built-in functions, such as print (). Also, we can create our own functions, that is, custom functions.

Next, look at a code:

// display(" * ")

// display(" *** ")

// display("*****")

If you need to output the above graphics in different parts of a program, it is not advisable to use the print () function to output each time. To improve writing efficiency and code reusability, we can organize code blocks with independent functions into a small module, which is called a function.

Defining Functions

We can define a function to achieve the desired functionality. Python definition functions begin with def, and the basic format for defining functions is as follows:

Def function {Enter the name here} (Enter parameters here):

"//Use this to define function String"

Function { Body}

Return expression

Note that if the parameter list contains more than one parameter, by default, the parameter values and parameter names match in the order defined in the function declaration.

Next, define a function that can complete printing information, as shown in Example below.

Example : Functions of Printing Information

defines a function that can print information.

def Useforprint():

print('-----------------------------------')

print ('life is short, I use python')

print('-----------------------------------')

Call Function

After defining a function, it is equivalent to having a piece of code with certain methods. To make these codes executable, you need to call it. Calling a function is very simple. You can call it by "function name ()".

For example, the code that calls the Useforprint function in the above section is as follows:

After the function is defined, the function will not be executed automatically and needs to be called

Useforprint()

Parameters of Function

Before introducing the parameters of the function, let's first solve a problem. For example, it is required to define a function that is used to calculate the sum of two numbers and print out the calculated results. Convert the above requirements into codes.

The sample codes are as follows:

def thisisaddition():

result = 62+12

print(result)

The functionality of the above function is to calculate the sum of 62 and 12. At this time, no matter how many times this function is called, the result will always be the same, and only the sum of two fixed numbers can be calculated, making this function very limited.

To make the defined function more general, that is, to calculate the sum of any two numbers, two parameters can be added when defining the function, and the two parameters can receive the value passed to the function.

Next, a case is used to demonstrate how a function passes parameters.

Example: Function Transfer Parameters

defines a function that receives 2 parameters

def thisisaddition(first, second):

third = first+second

print(third)

In Example, a function capable of receiving two parameters is defined. Where first is the first parameter for receiving the first value passed by the function; the second is the second parameter and receives the second value passed by the function. At this time, if you want to call the thisisaddition function, you need to pass two numeric values to the function's parameters.

The example code is as follows:

When calling a function with parameters, you need to pass data in parentheses.

thisisaddition(62, 12)

It should be noted that if a function defines multiple parameters, then when calling the function, the passed data should correspond to the defined parameters one by one.

Default Parameters

When defining a function, you can set a default value for its parameter, which is called the default parameter. When calling a function, because the default parameter has been assigned a value at the time of definition, it can be directly ignored, while other parameters must be passed in values. If the default parameter does not have an incoming value, the default value is directly used. If the default parameter passes in value, the new value passed in is used instead.

Next, we use a case to demonstrate the use of the default parameter.

Example : Default Parameters

```
def getdetails( input, time = 35 ):
# prints any incoming string
print("Details:", input)
print("Time:", time)
# calls printinfo function
printinfo(input="sydney" )
printinfo(input="sydney",time=2232)
```

In an example, lines 1-4 define the getdetails function with two parameters. Among them, the input parameter has no default value, and age has already set the default value as the default parameter.

When calling the getdetails function, because only the value of the name parameter is passed in, the program uses the default value of the age parameter. When the getdetails function is called on line 7, the values of the name and age parameters are passed in at the same time, so the program will use the new value passed to the age parameter.

It should be noted that parameters with default values must be located at the back of the parameter list. Otherwise, the program will report an error, for example, add parameter sex to the getdetails function and place it at the back of the parameter list to look at the error information.

With this, we have completed a thorough explanation of functions in python. In the next section, we will discuss different types of functions with an example.

Chapter 10: How to create own functions?

In this chapter, we are going to discuss various types of functions in detail. We will also in detail discuss user made functions with the help of an example.

According to whether there are parameters and return values, functions can be roughly divided into four types:

(1) The functions that have no parameters and no return value.

(2) The functions that have no parameters but returns a value.

(3) The function that has parameters but that doesn't return a value.

(4) Functions that have parameters and return values.

Next, the four types will be explained in detail.

Functions without Parameters and Return Values

Functions with no parameters and no return value can neither receive parameters nor return values.

Next, the use of this type of function is demonstrated by a function that prints prompts, as shown in Example.

Example: Functions Without Parameters and Return Values

def printresults():

// This is your place to choose

// display('Order your items here')

{ Now enter the output required for the entities}

printresults()

Functions with No Parameters but Returns Values

This type of function cannot receive parameters, but it can return some data. Generally, this type of function is used when collecting data. Next, we will demonstrate through an example.

Example: Functions with No Parameters but Returns Values

This will give temperature

def result():

Here are some processing procedures for obtaining temperature.

For the sake of simplicity, the simulation returns a data first.

 return 54

 usage = useresults()

print ('This is your body result', usage)

Functions with Parameters and No Return Value

In actual development, functions with parameters and no return value are rarely used. Because with functions as function modules and with parameters passed in, the return value is expected to be used in most cases. Here, everyone can know something about functions with parameters and no return value.

The example code is as follows:

```
// function
def send(usecase1,usecase2):
result=usecase1+usecase2
print ('calculated as: %d' %result)
```

Functions with Parameters and Return Values

Such functions can not only receive parameters but also return certain data. In general, such functions can be used for applications that process data and require results. Next, we will demonstrate it through a case.

Example: Functions with Parameters and Return Values

```
# calculates the cumulative sum of 1 ~ num
while i<=usetheresult:
result = result + i
i+=1
```

In the next section, we will describe user-made functions and will further explain the concept of user-made functions using a thorough example.

What is a user-made function?

A user made function is a function that creates a function with its parameters and logic. We usually have system functions such as print(), math() to solve a lot of day-to-day problems. User-made functions are usually used for repetitive tasks. In the next section, we will introduce you to a business card manager application that uses various user-made functions. Follow along to understand the essence of functions in programming.

Function Case- Business Card Manager

Business card manager is a practical software for life, which is used to help manage all business cards in mobile phones. To help people learn how to choose four types of functions in practical application, we develop a business card manager.

This case requires the use of functions to complete various functions, and according to the keyboard input to select the corresponding function to complete these functions.

There are six functions in the business card management menu, and the function selected by the user is responded by receiving the serial number input by the keyboard. Once the user enters "6", he will quit the business card management system.

First of all, Create a project and create a Python file named "Business Card Management System". The specific implementation steps are as follows.

1. Output the menu of the Business Card Manager

Considering that this function is only used to output information and the output content is fixed, a function displayMenu () with no parameters and no return value is defined as follows.

def display():

print("-"*60)

{ Enter the menu entities here}

```
print("-"*60)
```

Use the while loop to output menu information without interruption. To test the above menu function as soon as possible, the number of cycles is limited to 1, as follows.

```
first = 0
while first<1:
# Print menu
display()
```

Run the program and the console outputs the above menu information.

2. Obtain the information input by the user

After the menu is displayed, the user enters the serial number to be executed according to the prompt. The input () function receives the user's selection from the keyboard and returns the selected sequence number, so a function useinput() with no parameters and a return value is defined as follows.

```
# Get the information entered by the user
def useinput():
 storedvalue = input ("please enter the selected serial number:")
 return int(storedvalue)
```

After the while loop prints the menu, call the useinput () function to obtain the information entered by the user, as follows.

```
# Waiting for User Selection
present = useinput()
```

Run the program and the console outputs the information.

☐ *3. Perform different functions by obtaining serial numbers*

After obtaining the serial number, perform the corresponding operation according to the serial number. At the end of the while statement, use the if-Elif statement to complete the corresponding functions according to the sequence number selected by the user, as follows.

if present == 1:

pass

elif present == 2:

{Use the remaining conditional entities here}

print ("Incorrect input, please re-enter ...")

Next, the function corresponding to the serial number will be processed under each condition. Here, only the functions of "Add Business Card" and "Query Business Card" will be introduced.

4. Add Business Cards

To save all business card information, you need a list. Before the while statement, define an empty list as follows.

namespresent = []

The user has selected serial number 1, and should be prompted to enter his name and then add it to the above empty list. Therefore, we define a function with no parameters and no return value, as follows.

Add Business Cards

def enterInf():

enterInf = input ("please enter name:")

enterinf.append(newName)

Then, when the user selects the serial number 1, the above method is called to realize the function of adding business cards, as follows.

if present == 1:

enterInf()

elif present == 2:

Run the program and the console will output the information.

5.Check the information about all business cards

The user has selected serial number 5. At this time, all the name information should be obtained from the list and printed in a fixed format. Therefore, we define a function with parameters and no return value, as follows.

```python
# View information for all business cards
def getallnames(structure):
 print("="*60)
 for info in structure:
 print(info)
 print("="*60)
```

Then, when the user selects the serial number 5, the above method is called to realize the function of viewing all business cards, as follows.

```python
elif present == 4:
 pass
elif present == 5:
getallnames(nameList)
```

Run the program and the console will output the information.

With this, we have completed a brief explanation about user-made functions in Python. In the next chapter, we will start discussing conditional and loop statements in detail. Let us go!

Chapter 11: Conditional and Loops in Python?

In this chapter, we will learn in detail about conditional and loop statements. Before discussing these statements, we need to learn about judgment the essential concept required to master these concepts.

What is the judgment?

Judgment means that only when certain conditions are met one can be allowed to do something, while when the conditions are not met, one is not allowed to do it. For example, in real life, crossing the road depends on traffic lights. If it is a green light, you can cross the road, otherwise, you need to stop and wait.

Judgment is used not only in life but also in program development. For example, when a user logs in, only if the user name and password are all correct, he can be allowed to log in. Python provides many kinds of judgment statements. In the next section, we will explain these judgment statements in detail.

If statement

The if statement is the simplest conditional judgment statement. It can control the execution process of the program.

Its format is as follows:

If criteria:

Things to do when you meet the first condition.

Things to do when you meet the second condition

...

...

Things to be done when conditions are not met at all

In the above format, the following statement can be executed only if the judgment condition is satisfied.

□ To help people better understand the use of if statements, next, we will demonstrate the function of if statements through two cases, as follows.

Example:

//if statement -1

age=30

Print ("if judgment starts")

if age>=22:

Print ("This is true")

Print ("-if judgment ends")

In Example, the output of the program is different only if the value of the age variable is different. From this, we can see the function of if judgment statement that is: only when certain conditions are met the specified code will be executed, otherwise, it will not be executed.

Note:

1. Use a colon (:) after each if condition to indicate that the following statement is to be executed after the condition is met.

2. Use indents to divide statement blocks. Statements with the same number of indents together form a statement block.

3. There is no switch-case statement in Python.

if-else statement

When using if, it can only do what it wants to do when it meets the conditions. If it does not meet the conditions and needs to do something, what should it do? to counter this problem We can use if-else statements.

If-else statements are used in the following format:

If condition:

Things to do when you meet the first condition

Things to do when you meet the second condition.

...

Things to be done when nth conditions are met

else:

Things to do when the first conditions are not met

Things to do when second conditions are not met

...

Things to do when nth conditions are not met

To help people better understand the use of if-else statements, next, we will demonstrate the function of if-else statements through a case.

Example if-else statement

Ticket = 1 # with 1 for tickets, 0 for no tickets

if ticket == 1:

 print ("you can get on the train if you have a ticket")

 print ("I can finally see home")

else:

print ("No tickets, no boarding")

print ("Dear, I'll see you next time")

Set the value of the variable ticket to 0 and run the program again.

You will understand about conditional statements in depth if you can practice it by practical coding.

If nesting

When we take a train or subway, we have to buy a ticket first. Only when we buy a ticket, we can enter the station for security checks. Only when we pass the security check, we can take the bus normally. In the process of taking a train or subway, the latter judgment condition is based on the previous judgment. Given this situation, if nesting can be used.

If nesting refers to the inclusion of an if or if-else statement in an if or if-else statement, and its nesting format is as follows:

if conditions1:

{// What to do if condition 1 is met

  // things that meet condition 1

if conditions2:

things are done to meet condition 2

}

In the above format, we can choose whether to use if statement or if-else statement for the if of the outer layer and if of the inner layer according to the actual development.

Loop Statements

In real life, there are many cyclic procedures. For example, the alternation of traffic lights is a repetitive process. In the program, if you want to repeat some operations, you can use circular statements also called loops. Python provides two loop statements, the while loop and the for loop. We will now in detail discuss these two statements.

While loop

The basic format of the while loop is as follows:

While

{ Enter the logic

   Output results

}

If the condition is satisfied, the loop statement is executed.

When the conditional expression is True, the program executes a loop statement.

It should be noted that in the while loop, colon and indentation should also be noted. Also, there is no do-while loop in Python.

If we want the loop to be infinite, we can implement an infinite loop by setting the conditional expression to always be True. An infinite loop is very useful for real-time requests from clients on the server.

Next, a case is used to demonstrate the specific code.

Example: while loop

value = 1

While value == 1 :

expression is always True

 input = int(give ("enter a number:"))

 print ("The number you entered is:", input")

for loop

The for loop in Python can traverse any sequence of items, such as a list or a string.

The basic format of the for loop is as follows:

For variable in sequence:

loop statement

For example, use the for loop to traverse the list, the example code is as follows:

```
for result in [62,1,32]:
 print(result)
```

Output results:

62

1

32

In the above example, the for loop can display the values in the list one by one.

Considering that the range of values we use varies frequently, Python provides a built-in Range function that can generate a sequence of numbers.

The basic format of the range function in the for loop is as follows:

```
for result in range(get,set)
{
  Enter logic here
}
```

Execute loop statement

When the program executes the for loop, the loop timer variable result is set to start, and then the loop statement is executed. The result is sequentially set to all values between start and end. The loop statement is executed once for each new value set.

In an integer, the number divisible by 2 is called an even number. Now, we will develop a program to calculate the sum of even numbers between 1 and 100.

Example Calculate the Sum of Even Numbers from 1 to 100

first=0

Output=0

while i<101:

if first%2==0:

sum Output+=first

first+=1

Print ("the sum of even numbers between 1 and 100 is: %s" %first")

while nesting

It just represents a nested while in a while loop.

The while nesting format is as follows:

While condition 1:

When condition 1 is met, do 1

{

while condition 2:

When condition 2 is met, do 2

}

Relevant explanations of the above formats are as follows:

(1) When the loop condition 1 is satisfied, the things to be done when the condition 1 is satisfied are executed. At this time, there may be an opportunity to execute the loop nested inside.

(2) When the cycle condition 2 is satisfied, perform the things to be done when condition 2 is satisfied until the while cycle inside is finished.

(3) When the cycle condition 2 is not satisfied, the while cycle outside the loop is finished after the execution of the things to be done by the external loop.

With this, we have completed a brief discussion about conditionals and loops in Python. We will also discuss remaining control flow statements in the further chapter. For now, in the next chapter, we will in detail discuss object-oriented programming with a lot of examples.

Chapter 12: Object oriented programming in Python

There are various forms of things in the real world, and there are various connections between these things. In a program, objects are used to map real things and the relationships between objects are used to describe the relationships between things. This idea is the object-oriented paradigm.

When we talk about object-oriented programming, we naturally think of process-oriented programming. Process-oriented programming is to analyze the steps to solve the problem, and then use functions to implement these steps one by one when using different methods.

Object-oriented programming is to decompose the problem-solving entities into multiple objects, and the purpose of establishing objects is not to complete one by one but to describe the behavior of things in the process of solving the whole problem.

The following is an example of gobang to illustrate the difference between process-oriented and object-oriented programming.

First, use the process-oriented paradigm:

1. Start the game

2. Player 1 plays first

3. Draw the picture

4. Judges the result

5. Player 2 turn

6. Draw the picture

7. Judges the result

8. Return to Step 2

9. Output Final Results

The above steps are implemented by functions respectively, and the problem is solved using a process-oriented paradigm.

Object-oriented design solves the problem from another way of thinking. When using object-oriented thinking to realize gobang, the whole gobang game can be divided into three types of objects, as follows.

1. Black and White Parties: This represents the two players

2. Chessboard system: This is responsible for drawing pictures

3. Rule system: This is responsible for judging things such as foul, winning or losing, etc.

Among the above three-class objects, the first-class object (black and white parties) is responsible for receiving the user's input and notifying the second-class object (chessboard system) to draw pieces on the chessboard, while the third-class object (rule system) judges the chessboard.

Object-oriented programming ensures the unity of functions, thus making the code easier to maintain.

For example, if we want to add the function of chess now in a process-oriented paradigm, then a series of steps of input, judgment, and display needs to be changed. Even the loops between steps need to be adjusted on a large scale, which is very troublesome.

If object-oriented development is used, only the chessboard object needs to be changed. The chessboard object saves the chessboard scores of both black and white parties, and only needs simple backtracking, without changing the display and rules. At the same time, the calling sequence of the whole object function will not change, and its changes are only partial. Thus, compared with process-oriented, object-oriented programming is more convenient for later code maintenance and function expansion.

Classes and objects

In object-oriented programming, the two most important core concepts are class and object. Objects are concrete things in real life. They can be seen and touched. For example, the book you are holding is an object.

Compared with objects, classes are abstract, which is a general designation for a group of things with the same characteristics and behaviors. For example, when I was a child, my mother said to me, "Son, you should take that kind of person as an example!" The type of people here refers to a group of people who have excellent academic results and who are polite. They have the same characteristics, so they are called "same type" people.

Relationship between Class and Object

As the saying goes, "people are grouped by category, and things are grouped by group," we collectively refer to the collection of things with similar characteristics and behaviors as categories, such as animals, airplanes, etc.

For example, the toy model can be regarded as a class and each toy as an object, thus the relationship between the toy model and the toy can be regarded as the relationship between the class and the object. Class is used to describe the common features of multiple objects and is a template for objects. An object is used to describe individuals in reality. It is an instance of a class. As can be seen, objects are created according to classes, and one class can correspond to multiple objects.

Definition of Class

In daily life, to describe a kind of category, it is necessary to explain its characteristics as well as its uses. For example, when describing such entities as human beings, it is usually necessary to give a definition or name to such things. Human characteristics include height, weight, sex, occupation, etc. Human behaviors include running, speaking, etc. The combination of human characteristics and behaviors can completely describe human beings.

The design idea of an object-oriented program is based on this design, which includes the features and behaviors of things in classes. Among them, the characteristics of things are taken as the attributes of classes, the behaviors of things are taken as the methods of classes, and objects are an instance of classes. So to create an object, you need to define a class first. The class is composed of 3 parts.

(1) Class Name: The name of the class, whose initial letter must be uppercase, such as Person.

(2) Attribute: used to describe the characteristics of things, for example, people have the characteristics of name, age, etc.

(3) Method: Used to describe the behavior of things, for example, people have behaviors such as talking and smiling.

In Python, you can use the class keyword to declare a class with the following basic syntax format:

Class {Enter the entity here}:

This is property of a class

Method of class

The following is a sample code:

class Vehicle:

attribute

Method

 def drive(self):

Print ("-drivinf Automobile--")

In the above example, the class is used to define a class named Vehicle, in which there is a drive method. As can be seen from the example, the format of the method is the same as that of the function.

The main difference is that the method must explicitly declare a self-parameter and be located at the beginning of the parameter list. Self represents the instance of the class (object) itself, which can be used to refer to the attributes and methods of the object. The specific usage of self will be introduced later with practical application.

Creating Objects from Classes

If a program wants to complete specific functions, classes alone are not enough but also instance objects need to be created according to classes.

In Python programs, you can use the following syntax to create an object:

Object {Enter the entity name here } = Class { Enter the name here} ()

For example, create an object Vehicle of driving class with the following sample code:

vehicle = driving()

In the above code, vehicle is a variable that can be used to access the properties and methods of the class. To add attributes to an object, you can use the following syntax.

Object {Enter entity here}. New {Enter attribute name} = Value

For example, use vehicle to add the color attribute to an object of driving class.

The sample code is as follows:

vehicle.color = "black"

Next, a complete case is used to demonstrate how to create objects, add attributes and call methods. Look at it and clear all your doubts.

Example Sport.py

```
# Define Class
class Football:
# kick
def kick(goal):
print ("You scored ..." )
# Foul
def foul(self):
print ("You cheated" )
# creates an object and saves its reference with the variable BMW
Barcelona = Football()
# Add Attribute Representing Color
Barcelona.color = "blue"
# Call Method
Barcelona.goal()
Barcelona.foul()
# Access Attributes
print(Barcelona.color)
```

In Example, a Football class is defined, two methods kick and foul is defined in the class, then an object Barcelona of football class is created, color attribute is dynamically added and assigned to "blue", then goal () and foul () methods are called in turn, and the value of color attribute is printed out.

Structural Methods and Destructural Methods

In Python programs, two special methods are provided: __init__ () and __del__ (), which are respectively used to initialize the properties of the object and release the resources occupied by the class. This section mainly introduces these two methods in detail.

Construction method

In the previous example defining classes, we dynamically added the color attribute to the objects referenced by Barcelona. Just imagine, if you create another Football class object, you need to add attributes in the form of "object name. attribute name". For each object created, you need to add attributes once, which is very troublesome.

To solve this problem, attributes can be set when creating an object. Python provides a construction method with a fixed name of __init__ (two underscores begin and two underscores end). When creating an instance of a class, the system will automatically call the constructor to initialize the class.

To make everyone better understand, the following is a case to demonstrate how to use the construction method for initialization.

Example: uses the construction method. py

\# Define Class

class Football:

\# construction method

def __init__(kick):

Color = "blue"

\# Foul

def foul(self):

print ("%s Barcelona color is " (self.color))

creates an object and saves its reference with the variable car

football = Football()

football.foul()

In the example, lines 4-5 re-implemented the __init__ () method, adding the color attribute to the Football class and assigning it a value of "blue", and accessing the value of the color attribute in the foul method.

No matter how many Football objects are created, the initial value of the color attribute is "blue" by default. If you want to modify the default value of the property after the object is created, you can set the value of the property by passing parameters in the construction method.

The following is a case to demonstrate how to use the construction method with parameters.

Example: uses the parametric construction method. py

Define Class

class Football:

construction method

def __init__(kick):

Color = "blue"

Foul

def foul(self):

print ("%s Barcelona color is " (self.color))

creates an object and saves its reference with the variable car

football = Football()

football.foul()

creates an object and saves its reference with the variable bmw

realmadrid = color ("white")

realmadrid.color()

In Example, lines 4 to 5 customize the construction method with parameters, and assign the value of the parameters to the color attribute, ensuring that the value of the color attribute changes with the value received by the parameters, and then still access the value of the color attribute in the toot method.

Destructor Methods

Earlier, we introduced the __init__ () method. When an object is created, the Python interpreter will call the __init__ () method by default. When deleting an object to release the resources occupied by the class, the Python interpreter calls another method by default, which is the __del__ () method.

Next, a case is used to demonstrate how to use a destructor to release the occupied resources.

example: using destructor. py

```
# Define Class
class Football
  def __init__(team, color, name):
  team.name = name
  team.color = color
  def __del__(team):
  print("--------del--------")
Realmadrid = team ("white", 1)
```

In Example, a class named Person is defined, the initial values of color and team are set in the __init__ () method, a print statement is added in the __del__ () method, and then an object of the Person class is created using a custom construction method.

When the program ends, the memory space it occupies will be released.

So, can we release the space manually? Yes, Del statement can be used to delete an object and release the resources it occupies.

Add the following code at the end of Example:

```
del realmadrid
print("---------1---------")
```

☐ As you can observe from the results, the program outputs "del" before "1". This is because Python has an automatic garbage collection mechanism. When the Python program ends, the Python interpreter detects whether there is currently any memory space to be freed. If there is a del statement, it will be automatically deleted; if the del statement has been manually called, it will not be automatically deleted.

With this, we have given a thorough introduction to object-oriented programming in python. In the next chapter, we will talk about control flow statements in brief. Let us go!

Chapter 13: Control flow statements in Python

Previously we have discussed Conditionals and loop statements in detail. In this chapter, we will further continue discussing control statements briefly. A lot of examples are given to make you understand the essence of the topic. Let us dive into it.

What are the control flow statements?

All conditionals, loops and extra programming logic code that executes a logical structure are known as control flow statements. We already have an extensive introduction to conditionals and loops with various examples. Now, you should remember that the control flow statements we are going to learn now are very important for program execution. They can successfully skip or terminate or proceed with logic if used correctly. We will start learning about them now with examples. Let us go!

break statement

The break statement is used to end the entire loop (the current loop body) all at once. It is preceded by a logic.

for example, the following is a normal loop:

for sample in range(10):

print("-------")

print sample

After the above loop statement is executed, the program will output integers from 0 to 9 in sequence. The program will not stop running until the loop ends. At this time, if you want the program to output only numbers from 0 to 2, you need to end the loop at the specified time (after executing the third loop statement).

Next, demonstrate the process of ending the loop with a break.

Example: break Statement

end=1

for end in range(10):

end+=1

print("-------")

if end==3:

break

print(end)

In Example, when the program goes to the third cycle because the value of the end is 3, the program will stop and print the loop until then.

continue statement

The function of continue is to end this cycle and then execute the next cycle. It will look at the logical values and continue with the process.

Next, a case is used to demonstrate the use of the continue statement below.

Example continue statement

```
sample=1
for sample in range(10):
sample+=1
print("-------")
if sample==3:
continue
print(sample)
```

In Example, when the program executes the third cycle because the value of sample is 3, the program will terminate this cycle without outputting the value of sample and immediately execute the next cycle.

Note:

(1)break/continue can only be used in a cycle, otherwise, it cannot be used alone.

(2)break/continue only works on the nearest loop in nested loops.

pass statement

Pass in Python is an empty statement, which appears to maintain the integrity of the program structure. Pass does nothing and is generally used as a placeholder.

The pass statement is used as shown in Example below.

Example pass Statement

```
for alphabet in 'University':
 if letter == 'v':
 pass
 print ('This is the statement')
 print ('Use this alphabet', letter)
print ("You can never see me again" )
```

In Example above, when the program executes pass statements because pass is an empty statement, the program will ignore the statement and execute the statements in sequence.

else statement

Earlier, when learning if statements, else statements were found outside the scope of the if conditional syntax. In fact, in addition to judgment statements, while and for loops in Python can also use else statements. When used in a loop, the else statement is executed only after the loop is completed, that is, the break statement also skips the else statement block.

Next, we will demonstrate it through a case for your better understanding of the else block.

Example: else statement

```
result = 0
```

```
while result < 5:
 print(result, " is less than 5")
 result = result + 1
else:
 print(result, " is not less than 5")
```

In Example, the else statement is executed after the while loop is terminated, that is, when the value of the result is equal to 5, the program executes the else statement.

With this, we have completed a short introduction to control flow statements in Python programming. It is always important to use control flow statements only when they are necessary. □ If they are used without any use case, they may start creating unnecessary blockages while programming. In the next chapter, we will give a short introduction to decision trees in Python. Let us go!

Chapter 14: Decision trees in Python

In the previous chapter, we have discussed control flow statements and now we are going to discuss a concept that is related to control flow statements. Decision trees are a logical structure that can be used to make decisions based on certain criteria. A tree is a basic data structure that is usually used to store and sort things. We will now in detail discuss decision trees in python. Let us start!

What are decision trees?

Decision trees are a programming concept in python that can be used to make decisions. They are also used to make decisions based on the inputs given. Decision trees are mostly used in machine learning to create regression and supervised algorithms. We can implement decision trees in python using the pandas library that consists of a lot of algorithms.

In the next section, we will discuss the implementation of decision trees in detail. Follow along!

Implementation of decision trees

These decision trees usually work by depending on the questions that are asked on. If the logic that is given satisfies the condition then a decision is made. If it is not satisfied then it is passed onto the other node present.

How to select?

To select a node we need to operate as described below.

if (node logic)

{ If it statisfies

then save()

else

proceed.next()

The objective of this code is that the block of statement is checked upon by various complex logical entities. After completing the check if it is not satisfied then they will skip into the next node to perform the same operation. If they satisfy the condition the position value of the tree is stored in the error for further evaluation.

Installing decision tree in python

To install or work with decision trees you need to install pandas and ski-kit learn and use dependencies to use them. You can use pip to install them.

The format is here:

pip install {Enter the platform name here}

Algorithm of the decision tree

For any data structure, it is important to follow the algorithm that has been mentioned. Now, we will in detail explain the decision tree algorithm according to the python programming language. Follow along!

Step 1:

At first, you need to consider all the data that is present as a root set.

Step 2:

In the next step, you need to understand the attributes that are present and should need to work on parameters to display the results.

Step 3:

In this step, you need to perform recursive operations on the values that you have used for the comparison.

Step 4:

In the last step, you need to use different statistical and pseudo methods to understand the node calculations.

Data import for decision trees

To import data that works on decision trees you need to use pandas third-party library. You can either fetch the URL details or you can use CSV format to send information. You can even use the import statement to get the task done.

Data slicing for decision trees

It is often hard to send a lot of information to the decision tree at once. To counter this problem python provides data slicing operations where the data can be divided according to your requirement.

To perform excellent decision tree operations, it is important to master complex computer science topics such as the Gini Index, Entropy which are out of the scope of this book. If you are interested to construct your own decision tree algorithms, we recommend you to learn in-depth about the Information gain mechanism.

With this, we have completed a brief explanation about decision trees in Python. In the next chapter, we will learn about exception handling in detail. Let us go!

Chapter 15: Essential programming in Python

In python, it is essential to deal with errors to make programs run. Whenever a python program stops running for the user due to warnings and errors it is advised to show the reasons for the end-user. Python programmers should develop this skill by understanding the essence of exception handling in python. It is very essential for making things work smoothly. In this chapter, we will discuss this in detail with examples. Let us start!

Brief Introduction of Anomalies

In Python, errors generated during the execution of a program are called exceptions, such as list indexes crossing boundaries, opening files that do not exist, etc.

For example, an error occurs when running the following program code.

open(data.txt)

FileNotFound { There is no such file: 'data.txt' }

Abnormal Class

In Python, all Exception classes are subclasses of Exception. The exceptions class is defined in the Exceptions module, which is in Python's built-in namespace and can be used directly without import.

In the previous chapters, the program threw an exception every time it encountered an error in executing the program. If the exception object is not processed and captured, the program will terminate execution with a traceback, which includes the name of the error (such as NameError), the reason and the line number where the error occurred.

Here are some common exceptions.

1.NameError

Attempting to access an undeclared variable raises a NameError.

For example:

print(dude)

The error message is as follows:

NameError: There is no such namespace

The above information indicates that the interpreter did not find foo in any namespace.

2.ZeroDivisionError

When the divisor is zero, a ZeroDivisionError exception is thrown.

For example:

1/0

The error message is as follows:

ZeroDivisionError: division by zero is not possible

Any numerical value divided by zero will lead to the above exception.

3.SyntaxError

When the interpreter finds a SyntaxError, it will throw a syntax error exception.

For example:

list = ["two","four","six"]

for result in list

 print(result)

In the above example, due to the lack of a colon after the for loop, the program has the following error message:

SyntaxError: This is not the correct syntax

The SyntaxError exception is the only exception that does not occur at runtime. It represents an incorrect structure in Python code that prevents the program from executing. These errors generally occur at compile-time, and the interpreter cannot convert the script into byte code.

4.IndexError

An IndexError exception is thrown when using an index that does not exist in the sequence.

For example:

example = []

example[0]

In the above example, there is no element in the list. When accessing the first element of the list with index 0, the following error message appears:

IndexError: There is no such index

The above information indicates that the index value of the list is beyond the range of the list.

5.KeyError

When using a key that does not exist in the map, a KeyError exception is thrown.

For example:

Thisresult = {'number':'explain','port':7232}

Thisresult['interpret']

In the above example, there are only two keys host and port in myDict dictionary. When obtaining the corresponding value of the interpret key, the following error message appears:

KeyError: 'interpret'

The above information indicates that there is a key server that does not exist in the dictionary.

6.FileNotFoundError

When trying to open a file that does not exist, a file not found IOError exception is thrown.

For example:

second = open("test")

In the above example, using the open method to open a file or directory named test, the following error message appears:

FileNotFoundError: { There is nothing that exists with this name}

The above information indicates that no file or directory named test was found.

7.AttributeError

An AttributeError exception is thrown when attempting to access an unknown object attribute.

For example:

class Aeroplane(object):

fly

flight = Aeroplane()

Aeroplane.color = "white"

In the above example, the Aeroplane class does not define any attributes and methods. After creating an instance of the Aeroplane class, the color attribute is dynamically added to the instance referenced by the flight, and then the following error message appears when accessing it's color and name attributes:

AttributeError: 'Aeroplane' object has no attribute 'value'

The above information indicates that the color attribute is defined in the Aeroplane instance, so it can be accessed by flight.color. However, the name attribute is not defined, so an error occurs when accessing the name attribute.

In the next section, we will discuss exception handling in detail. Follow along!

Exception handling

Python's ability to handle exceptions is very powerful. It can accurately feedback error information and help developers to accurately locate the location and cause of problems. Try-except statements are used in Python to handle exceptions. Among them, try statements are used to detect exceptions and exception statements are used to catch exceptions.

Capture Simple Exceptions

The try-except statement defines a piece of code to monitor exceptions and provides a mechanism to handle exceptions.

The simplest try-except statement format is as follows:

try :

Here is the place where logic goes

except :

Here we enter the error details

When an error occurs in a statement in a try block, the program will no longer continue to execute the statement in the try block, but will directly execute the statement that handles the exception in exception.

To make readers better understand, the following is a case to demonstrate how to use a simple try-except statement to try to capture the possible exceptions caused by dividing two numbers, as shown in the example.

Example: Simple Exceptions. py

```
try:
print("-"*64)
first = input ("You should enter the first entity")
second = input ("You should enter the second entity")
print(int(first)/int(second))
print("-"*64)
except ZeroDivisionError:
print ("Number 64 cannot be divided")
```

In Example, two values input by the user are received in the input function of the try clause, wherein the first value is taken as the dividend and the other value is taken as the divisor. If the divisor is 0, the program will throw a ZeroDivisionError exception. In this case, the exception clause will catch the exception and print the exception information.

Run the program and enter the first number of 64 and the second number of 5 in the console. The result will be shown. By analyzing this carefully you will understand how exception handling works.

From the results, it can be seen that when the program is abnormal, the program will not be terminated again, but the user will be reminded according to the message set by himself. Note that as long as errors are monitored, the program will execute the statements except and will no longer execute the unexecuted statements in a try.

Capture the description information of the anomaly

Multiple exceptions can be caught through an except clause. The two errors of Example are combined into an except clause as follows.

try:

 first = input ("Enter the first entity")

 second = input ("Enter the second entity")

 print(int(first)/int(second))

except (ZeroDivisionError, Enter the value here):

 print ("Get a value")

At this time, no matter anyone of the above two exceptions occurs, the statement inside the exception will be printed. However, printing only one error message is not helpful. To distinguish different error information, as can be used to obtain error information fed back by the system.

Capture all abnormalities

Even if the program can handle multiple exceptions, it is impossible to prevent them, and, likely, some exceptions are still not caught. In Example, if num1 is written as nmn1 when writing the program, an error message similar to the following will be obtained.

NameError: name 'nmn1' is not defined

In such a case, the SyntaxError exception can be captured on the original basis. If there are dozens of errors in the program, it is very troublesome to catch these exceptions. To solve this situation, the exception clause can not specify the exception type, so it can handle any type of exception.

To make readers understand better, the function of capturing all abnormalities is added as an example here.

Example: Captures All Exceptions

```
# captures all exceptions
try:
first = input ("Use this as first entity")
second = input ("Use this as second entity")
print(int(first)/int(second))
except :
print ("You got this error")
```

In Example, the except statement does not indicate the type of exception, and all possible errors of the program are uniformly handled in the statement.

As can be seen from the results of the two runs, the prompt information for all exceptions is the same. Another way to catch all Exceptions is to use the exception class after the exception statement. Since the Exception class is the parent of all exception classes, all exceptions can be caught.

No exception was caught

In the if statement, when all the conditions are not met, the else statement is executed. Similarly, if the try statement does not capture any error information, it will not execute any exception statement but will execute the else statement.

To make readers understand better, we add else statement based on the above example.

Example else statement. py

```
try:
first = input ("Use this as first entity")
second = input ("Use this as second entity")
print(int(first)/int(second))
except :
print ("You got this error")
else:
```

print ("The program runs normally and no exception is caught")

In Example, when an error is detected in the try statement, the printing statement in except will be executed and the description information of the exception will be output. When there is no error, the print statement in else will be executed.

With this, we have completed a brief explanation of essential programming concepts. In the next chapter, we will discuss file management in detail. Follow along!

Chapter 16: File management in Python

Python is a programming language that deals with a lot of file operations in general. It has a special library to deal with file management functionalities. This chapter is a comprehensive introduction to all of the file management methods that are available in python. We also provided python programming code statements for your further analysis. Let us start!

Opening and Closing of Files

Let's imagine, if you want to use a word document to write a resume, what should be the process?

(1) Open Word document software and create a new file.

(2) Write personal resume information.

(3) save the file.

(4) Close Word document software.

Similarly, the overall process of manipulating files in Python is very similar to the process of writing a resume using Word.

(1) Open a file or create a new one.

(2) Read/write data.

(3) close the file.

Next, we will introduce the opening and closing of files respectively.

Opening of Files

In Python, the open method is used to open a file in the following syntax format:

Open (Name of the file [access mode information])

In the above format, the filename must be filled in, and information about access mode is optional (access mode will be described in detail later in this chapter).

For example, open a file named "country.txt" with the following sample code:

entity = open('country.txt')

It should be noted that if the access mode is not specified when opening the file by using the open method, the file must be guaranteed to exist, otherwise, the following abnormal information will be reported.

FileNotFound { // We are unable to find the file specified}

Document Mode

If you use the open method to open a file with only one file name, then we can only read one file. If the open file allows writing data, the mode of the file must be indicated. There are many access modes for files in Python.

"RB", "WB" and "AB" modes all operate files in binary mode. Usually, these modes are used to process files of binary types, such as sound or image.

Closing of Documents

Always use the close method to close open files. Even if a file will be automatically closed after the program exits, considering the safety of the data, the close method should be used to close the file after each use of the file. Otherwise, once the program crashes, the data in the file may not be saved.

The close method is very simple to use, with specific examples as follows:

Create a new file with the file name country.txt

sample = open('country.txt', 'w')

Close this file

sample.close()

Reading and writing of documents

The most important ability of a file is to receive data or provide data. The reading and writing of files is nothing more than writing data into or reading data from files. Next, this section will explain the reading and writing of files respectively.

Writing Documents

Writing data to a file needs to be completed by using the write method. when operating a file, every time the write method is called, the written data will be appended to the end of the file.

Example: Writing Data to Files

f = open('data.txt', 'w')

f.write('This is an example for writing data')

f.close()

After the program runs, a file named data.txt will be generated under the path where the program is located. Open the file and you can see that the data was successfully written.

Note:

When writing data to a file, if the file does not exist, the system will automatically create a file and write the data. If the file exists, the data of the original file will be emptied and the new data will be rewritten.

Reading documents

When reading data from a file, it can be obtained in a variety of ways, as follows.

1. Use the read method to read the file

The read method can read data from a file, and its definition syntax is as follows:

read(size)

In the above method, the size represents the length of data to be read from the file, in bytes. If the size is not specified, then all data of the file is read.

Example: Use read Method to Read Files

example = open('data.txt', 'r')

value = f.read(22)

value = f.read()

2. Use the readlines method to read files

If the content of the file is very small, you can use the readlines method to read the content of the entire file at one time. The readlines method returns a list with each element in the list being each row of data in the file. Suppose the file "data. txt" contains three lines of data then the way to read the file using the readlines method is shown in the example below.

Example: Use the readlines Method to Read Files

sample = open('data.txt', 'r') 2 entity = f.readlines()

☐ *Application of File Reading and Writing-Making Backup of Files*

In actual development, the reading and writing of files can accomplish many functions. For example, the back up of files is the process of reading and writing files.

☐ At this time, if you want to make a backup file of data.txt, you need to read the data of the original file and write the acquired data into the backup file. Compared with the original file, the backup file stores the same data as the original file.

Example: Making a Backup of Files

secondfile = firstfile [result]+'[copy]'+data]

secondfile= open(secondfilename, 'w')

for instance in firstfile.readlines():

secondfile.write(lineContent)

Positioning, Reading, and Writing of Files

In the previous study, the reading and writing of documents were all done in sequence. However, in actual development, it may be necessary to start reading and writing from a specific location of the file. At this time, we need to locate the reading and writing location of the file, including obtaining the current reading and writing location of the file and locating the specified reading and writing location of the file.

In the next section, the two positioning methods are introduced in detail as follows.

1. Use the tell method to obtain the current read-write location of the file

In the process of reading and writing files, if you want to know the current location, you can use the tell method to get it. The tell method returns the current location of the file, that is, the current location of the file pointer.

Example: Use tell Method to Obtain the Current Read and Write Location of Files

place = get.tell()

print ("Required position:", place ")

value = set.read(3)

print ("The data read is:", str ")

Find Position of the page

place = find.tell()

2. Use the seek method to locate the specified read-write location of the file

If it is necessary during the process of reading and writing files to start reading and writing from the specified location, you can use the seek method.

The syntax for defining the seek method is as follows:

seek(offset[whence])

The parameters of the seek method are described below.

(1)offset: Indicates the offset, that is, the number of bytes to be moved.

(2)whence indicates the direction.

There are three values for this parameter:

(1) The default value of Seek _ Set or 0: Whence parameter indicates offset from the starting position of the file.

(2) seek _ cur or 1: indicates offset from the current position of the file

(3) seek _ end or 2: offset from the end of the file.

Example: Use the seek method to locate the specified location of the file

value.seek(4)

Find Current position

place=get.tell()

print ("the current file location is:", position ")

Renaming and Deleting Files

Sometimes, files need to be renamed and deleted. Python's os module already includes these functions by default.

Next, this section will explain the renaming and deletion of files in detail.

Renaming of Files

The rename method of the os module can complete the renaming of files in the following format:

os.rename(Nameofthesource,dst)

In the above format, src refers to the file name to be modified, dst refers to the modified new file name.

For example, the example code for renaming the file "Hotel. txt" to "Restaurant" is as follows:

import os

Os.rename ("hotel. txt", "restaurant. txt")

Deletion of documents

The remove method of the os module can complete the deletion of files in the following format:

os.remove(path)

In the above format, path refers to the file under the specified path.

For example, the example code for deleting the file "Tour. txt" under the current path is as follows:

import os

os.remove ("tour. txt")

Folder operations

In the actual development, it is sometimes necessary to operate the folder in a program way, such as creating and deleting. Just as the os module is required for file operation, the os module is also required for folder operation. In the next section, the creation of the folder, the acquisition of the current directory, the change of the default directory of the file and the deletion of the folder will be explained as follows.

1. Create a folder

The mkdir method of the os module is used to create folders, and the example code is as follows:

import os

Os.mkdir ("Executive")

2. Get the current directory

The getcwd method of os module is used to obtain the current directory.

The sample code is as follows:

import os

os.{Get the current directory}()

3. Change the default directory

The chdir method of the os module is used to change the default directory, for example, the code for changing the current directory to the directory at the next higher level is as follows:

import os

os.chdir("../")

4. Get the directory list

The listdir method of os module is used to obtain the directory list. For example, to obtain the subdirectory list under the current path, the code is as follows:

import os

os.listdir("./")

5. Delete the folder

The rmdir method of the os module is used to delete folders. For example, the following code deletes the "Executive" directory under the current path:

import os

Os.rmdir ("Executive")

With this, we have completed a brief and detailed explanation to the file management system in Python. With this, we have completed a deep journey into the Python universe. Now, it's time for you to implement these concepts in real-world programming. All the best!

Conclusion

Glad that you have reached the end of this book. I hope you have enjoyed the content provided in the book as much we loved making this book.

What to do next?

As you have completed a complex and thorough book that deals with Python programming it is now a huge test for you to apply your programming skills on real time projects. There are a lot of open-source projects that are waiting for a contribution. Remember that reading a lot of Python code will also help you understand the programming logics that python possesses.

That's it! Thanks for purchasing this book again and All the best!